# HOW WE MOVE TOWARD LIGHT

# HOW WE MOVE TOWARD LIGHT

New & Selected Poems

Michael Magee

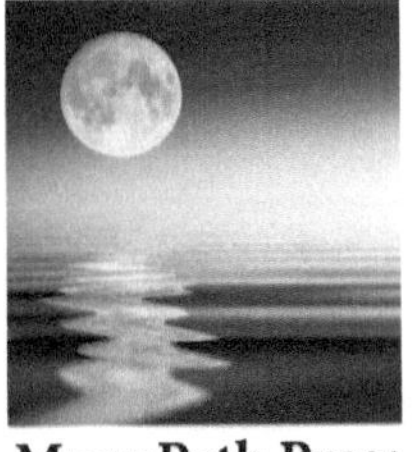

MoonPath Press

Poetry
ISBN 978-1-936657-40-7

Cover art: "Summer Sunrise" by artist Christine Karron Originally from Estonia and Germany, Karron is a Canadian illustrator and painter. She is the author of coloring books and the creator of Benny Blue (Rabbit). She says, "Swirl shapes are symbolic for spirits of the Universe." Visit her online @ http://chkarron.com/

Author photo: by Eleana Pawl

Design: Tonya Namura Gentium Book Basic

MoonPath Press is dedicated to publishing the finest poets of the U.S. Pacific Northwest.

MoonPath Press
PO Box 445
Tillamook, OR 97141

MoonPathPress@gmail.com

http://MoonPathPress.com

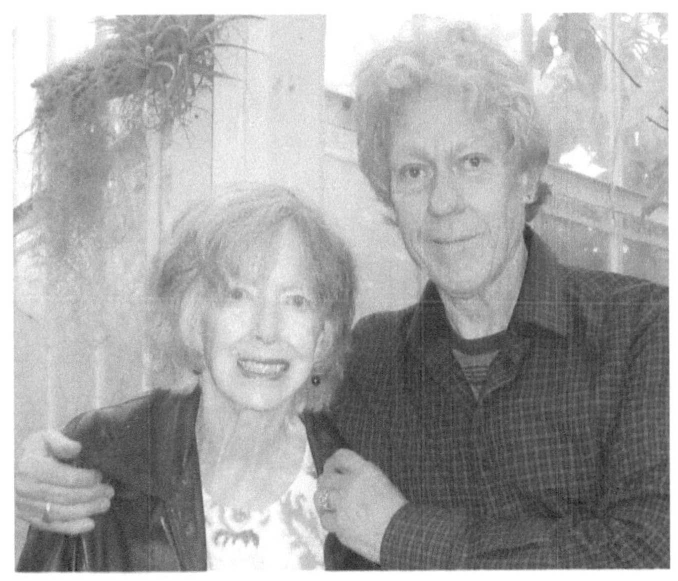

*In memory of my wife, Jean*

(1928-2018)

In the stiff pages of your book
I read my own heart, folded there
a message for you, that in love,
we find mystery, roses growing up
a trellis, and so we find our shape
in art.

# ACKNOWLEDGMENTS

Grateful acknowledgment to the publications that published many of the poems in this collection, sometimes in earlier versions. And thanks to the organizations that conferred awards to several of the poems in this collection.

**Publications:**

*20/20: Tacoma In Images and Verse:* "Oyster Light"

*360 Gallery:* "Samba Sentimental"

*4th Street Umbrella:* "At Chief Sealth's Grave, Suquamish"

*A Trip to Jerusalem:* "The Return of Odysseus"

*Arnazella:* "Chinese Character"

*The Arts:* "The Ventriloquist"

*The Avocet:* "I Saw Walt Whitman in Wright Park"

*Crab Creek Review:* "Elegy for Ariel"

*Epoch:* "The Man Who Broke into Song"

*Hotchpotch:* "Contours"

*In Tahoma's Shadow Anthology:* "Icarus Rising"

*Jack Straw Writer's Anthology:* "Curkarna," "Remembered Light," "Picasso at 90," "Firenze Remembered"

*Journal of Wild Culture:* "Portway Tavern, on the Columbia," "Van Gogh's Opening Pitch," "My Father's Driftwood," "The Giants of Astoria"

*Low Over Gratiot Road:* "Compost Heap"

*Mélange:* "The Long Room at Trinity College"

*Mute Note Earthward Anthology:* "Chagall's Dream"

*Moonthorn Tapestry:* "Cambiare La Casa"

*Of Sun and Sand Anthology:* "Solzhenitsyn at the Beach"

*Only Connect:* "St. Nicholas of Turkey"

*Pennine Ink:* "Love's a Blur"

*Perceptions:* "Flamin' June"

*Petals in the Pan Anthology:* "Bouquet," "Take Time to Steal the Lilacs"

*Poetry Atlas.Com:* "Mark This Wall," "Sheep Grazing at Vindolanda," "Bella and Me on Mt. Rushmore," "Little Chapel in Wall Drugs, South Dakota"

*Poetry Chicago:* "It Is the Stars That Govern us"

*Poetry Northwest:* "The Rainbow"

*Poets West Literary Journal:* "Masaccio's Expulsion of Adam and Eve," "*Il Volto Santo*: The Black Christ of Lucca," "Waiting for The Last Supper, Santa Maria Della Grazie," "Fratelli's Cows," "Ginger Autumn," "Mary, Mary and Jack the Lad," "Rapunzel," "How Carrie Howard's Daughter Learned to Love 'Da' Moon," "Harry Potter and the Midnight Express"

*Pyrokinection:* "Odysseus at the Mall"

*Real Change:* "Odysseus in the Land of Toaster Ovens," "Pathogenesis"

*Sand and Sea Anthology:* "Volare' 1958"

*Seattle Review:* "Walking Papers"

*Secrets and Dreams Anthology:* "Swan Upping"

*Staxtes Greek Literary Journal:* "Odysseus at Rest," "Prologue: Odysseus and the Eclipse," "Odysseus on Hydra"

*Storm Cycle Anthology 2015:* "Proust in the Park"

**Awards:**

"Chagall's Dream": First Prize, Dancing Poetry
Festival, San Francisco

"Proust in the Park": Second Prize, Editor's Choice
Awards, KindofaHurricaine Press

"Remembered Light": First Prize, City of Tacoma

"Sitting at the Sylvia Beach Memorial Reading Room,
Shakespeare and Co., Paris": Wellberry Prize, First
Place

# TABLE OF CONTENTS

# HOW WE MOVE
# TOWARD LIGHT

"How do you paint wind?"
"Ah! By making the trees go whiz-bang and whoop it
up. By painting in thick vigorous swirls."

—from *The Forest Lover*,
a novel about Emily Carr,
by Susan Vreeland

# INTRODUCTION

In the crazy years of the late Sixties, sometimes with the whiff of tear gas still in the air, I came to know Michael Magee over the poetry of John Donne in a class I then taught at the University of Washington. More than forty years later we picked up again. What he has made of his world over these intervening decades, and what seem like several different worlds, is brought together in the many poems collected here in *How We Move Toward Light*.

The mood and scope of the whole are sounded in Part I, The New Odysseus, a series of twenty linked poems, where a somewhat weary new Odysseus invokes his legendary adventures and various gods as he wanders both in the Tacoma present and yet in other lands and times, with an eye on our absurd world of the coffee house, sex change, the mall, pogo sticks, an anomalous game of cricket, poverty, yearning, old age, mortality, a quiet, bleak fading. It is a phantasmagorical trip, told with a kind of rueful even solemn whimsy which is his own.

The following two sections reflect Magee's personal odyssey. They give us back the varied worlds he has inhabited, their landscapes and meanings, through the vision of artists and poets whose personae Magee explores and at times adopts. It is a strange world, steeped in art, populated by the active ghosts of Proust, Whitman, Roethke, Chagall, O'Keeffe, Yeats, Cather and others, as well as by spirits like Rapunzel. But then a homeless man speaks as he wakes in his cold blankets near Seattle docks. Or we pause in front of a Dali painting to consider time itself. It is quite a trip.

The book is dedicated to Jean Musser, the poet's late
wife and fellow poet. She also appears movingly in a
few of the poems. Her presence is felt throughout.


—Ben Drake

# HOW WE MOVE TOWARD LIGHT

The new Thundercloud Plum
is awakening through the degrees
of the debris of an afterlife
from December storms, its popcorn
blossoms giving off the sun
where it opens near the American
Sweetgum, English Field Maple.

How we move toward the light
learning the names of things
that no one ever told us.
We discover our own limbs when
out of the death of winter comes
a new season we can call our own.

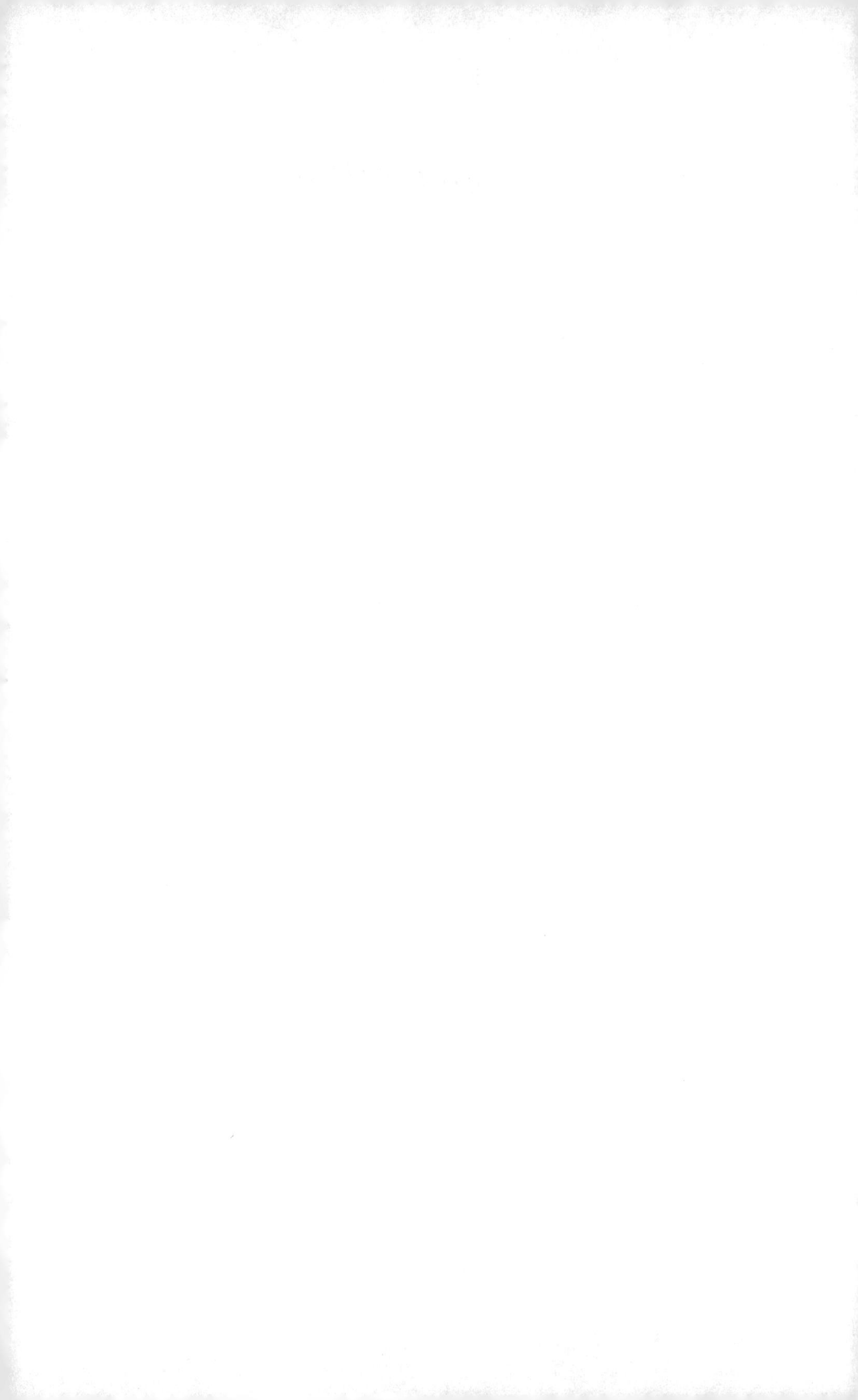

I beg you muses to inspire me
to write this rhapsody.
—Homer

# I
# THE NEW ODYSSEUS

# PROLOGUE: ODYSSEUS AND THE ECLIPSE

"Homecoming of Odysseus may have been
in Eclipse"

—*New York Times*

As Odysseus traveled the world
   got darker
all along the path of his eclipse
   evening deepened
left in tatters all the worse
his warrior's heart was broken.

No longer beating for war
he dreamed of Penelope, Telemachus
   his only son
his words unstrung, his ship and crew
   destroyed
he wandered the Aegean like a swallow
   off its course.

Looking for stars to guide him
   bribed and borrowed and battered crew
    cut loose
across the Ionian Sea with a new moon
   to mark this verse.
Come stay awhile to hear my sorrow.

Except for war Odysseus would be home:
   no more ambrosia, no more Circe
no more siren-song, or the giant Cyclops
   not on the rocks, just a memory
meandering his way home to Ithaca.

The birds no longer sang
  their mixolydian melodies, depressed
at so many ill omens, prophecy
  that filled him with dread
a penumbra filled his head
  craving of his heartache.

In this twilight, he waxed and waned
the beard that weighed him down
his hair filled with eels,
his eyes always staring ahead
toward a flat-screen horizon.

# THE RETURN OF ODYSSEUS

My head is empty now, of all suffering
as I leave London,
compression brakes squealing,
the steel-splitting rails.

In Midland Industrial England
I am passing the time, nodding
through green grocer's fields,
a pleasant relief from the wars.

Somewhere, a memory of siren sleep.
I am hopeful, open-hearted
in this land of blank canvas,
a landscape still to be gessoed.

With no dreams to be shattered
in my Moroccan mirror, I can examine
the shiny, dented teapot I drank
tea-de-menthe from in Marrakech.

I have come through all of this,
having missed my flight from Malaga,
taking the last boat home from Tangier
on time and unrehearsed.

No loose threads
a family dead and gone, longing
for my wife and children
in a place I have no place.

# ODYSSEUS AND THE SEA CHANGE

"I'm changed" just like the old ballad
after temptation, storms, my enigmas
here I am in a mid-sea-life crisis, not knowing
whether I should go back or forward.
Instead, I'm plagued with memories of
Penelope, and all my battles in the past.
Now, what's a warrior without a war
to fight? This will take getting used to—
constantly at sea between Charybdis and Scylla,
how can I steer a middle ground:
"Valor" all those hollow words.
With my receding hairline and love handles
what's left but this stream of consciousness?

# ODYSSEUS ON HIS WATERBED

How long since I have known the wine-dark
sea, the inflatable mattress with mallards on it
its ever-changing currents that flow
beneath me. Long since I slept on a mattress
and box spring; that was in another dream.
Here the surface washes under me, and warm
I lie in a Mediterranean sponge tide.
Once I had to climb up, now, I collapse
into the rolling, spreading jellyfish of sleep
that transports me, far from my animal skin
into the swells of a life without bed springs
while I lie on my moss-green sea of strife.

## ODYSSEUS ON HYDRA

On a Greek Island floating
in the Saronic Gulf,
the hydra-headed monster
has been replaced by windmills,
and the donkeys bray to us
like they're laughing at sunrise.

Tourists swim like sea-turtles,
sunning themselves, naked
on the rocks, below the white walls
of Hydra that tell us we
have all been lost.

Bougainvillea follows us,
flourish of the slipper parade at dusk,
dolphins, lovers of Zeus
sport in the sea, banished long ago
by Hera.

While grey-eyed Pallas Athena still
watches, patron of Athens to keep
us from falling overboard as we ride
on the Flying Dolphin.

I've come here wanting to drift,
across the Peloponnesus,
no odes to write, no loom, so I'm
not ready to be found yet, still looking
for a few good goddesses.

# ODYSSEUS IN A LAND OF POGO STICKS

Men with pogo sticks more than
        you can shake a stick at
crazy with their jumping
        up and down
like bean counters with St. Vitus Dance
        make me wonder at
man's inhumanity to the land.
How can we push the dimpled pole,
impress ourselves into the earth,
until we hop into our holes
who don't know when to stop
jumping, sit astride our sensible
        selves.
O, Men you are only the sad relics
of leapfrogs.

## ODYSSEUS IN A LAND OF TOASTER OVENS

So many crumbs, so little time
I feel the red glow the filaments
        in my own chest
like English muffins in apprenticeship
        warm and warmer
they have suckled a generation
        of hybrids
those who have never known
the exasperation of a pop-up toaster.

In my memory bank, long ago,
the spring recoiled in some
far-off mechanical dreams
        but now
with these toaster ovens, there is
no pushing down, only the laying on
of butter and jam as the racks warm
those who sun themselves on grills.

How I miss the long accruing toaster
instead, a world of the horizontal
has overtaken our vertical reach.
We can only stack them high with
        little thought. O forgive us!

# ODYSSEUS ON THE SUNFLOWER ISLANDS

On the islands' soft margins,
we bicycle around on tripods,
always looking for oyster shells
to get drunk from.

The people here are friendly,
waving their worn fishing nets
like old G-strings at us,
having caught too many raindrops.

They grow strong and tall,
bending their necks with flat
Cycladic faces, and a long bridge
to their breakwater noses.

They speak in perpetual sing-song.
"Who talks to us," they say.
At night they simply fold into shadows
while dreaming of lions.

During the long daytime, they sway
in long conga lines, attached
to a tow rope like notes, slaves
on a musical stave.

Their heads bob up and down
to the beat of the conch shells.
Whenever I see them, I find
these spots before my eyes.

## ODYSSEUS AND REVLON, MAYBELLINE IN THE LAND OF MAKE BELIEVE

Ice blue with a rare pink blush,
her cosmetic pad lies in its powdery bed
entices us with pale iris blue eyes,
mouth shaped like a tortoise shell,
long-lashed like a tropical storm
that plays upon our vainest hope.
We are reduced to staring at them.

Bright blue eyes belie the hidden motive
beneath their mascara and eye shadow,
the pale shadowy-moon-of the face
with Revlon Overstay lip color and balm.
Rising out of dreams salad-tossed with
stark surprise, the Janet Leigh wide-eyed
look in a dream staring openly giving us

no place to hide our manly arts; instead
we fall helpless to the eye-liner, pencil,
the cosmetic brush and retractable gloss.
Is it only a mask or pancake make-up?
Can we believe in what we see, or
is it a delusion of cosmetic surgery, this
appearance, chimera rouge of femininity.

# ODYSSEUS AMONG THE
AMBROSIA PETALS

I thought that here perhaps
I could rest among the blossoms
without sex rearing its ugly head
until suddenly I could feel
a sweetness taking hold.

Maybe I could put down my aegis
for once, relax and not worry
about being the faithful husband,
even wondering about Penelope
and if there would be a homecoming.

But in the meantime,
she wasn't here and the perfume
was everywhere while nymphs were
rearranging themselves among
spears of wild lavender.

The ambrosia made me giddy
and I dropped all caution
looked for a place to lie down.
Maybe a roll in the clay
wouldn't be so bad after all.

So I gave myself poetic license.
O Circe, you turned my men into pigs.
Could you care for an older man?
I clasped her beautiful knees
and prayed for a favorable wind.

# ODYSSEUS IN THE LAND OF
# LETTUCE EATERS

I don't like being a vegetarian
give me red meat to kill,
and a pair of drumsticks,
or some kippered barbarian,
a French Dip with au jus.

When you're in a far-off place,
you need lots of protein
for hand to hand combat.
There's nothing quite as tasty
as a plate of fresh Mesopotamians.

Or nothing like an Irish stew
made with real Celts,
and Abyssinian beef jerky,
or a nice Saracen stir-fry.
The rest is for your salad days.

# ODYSSEUS IN A LAND OF WALLFLOWERS

Nap time, their fingers
twitch like they're
picking blackberries
and the muffled talk
as though they are
speaking through socks.

At your table
coffins are dusted off.
Some lying in wait
are unplugged by now,
others rest, their heads
on their laptops, like they are
shiny pillows.

But leave no dents
in their heads, their legs
dangle like chopsticks
wobbling over a rice bowl
of fresh sushi. Finally, they
are falling asleep over
and fading into dotcoms.

## ODYSSEUS ON THE RETURN VOYAGE, SECOND LEG TEST MATCH WITH THE OTHER SIDE OUT

It came from my side split like a wooden bat
after the Trojan War, I didn't know who my
friends or enemies were anymore.
So, I slept away, lost my crew and crown
to the Hydra-headed monster, a leg-spinner.
Washed up on the shore to be tempted
by yet another Circe, I finally escaped the run out
no LBW, but resumed batting, piling up 100 runs
kissed a sailor, floated on a pea-green bark
all the way to Ithaca where I found my son, my life
and faithful dog, pledged myself to family values,
slew a household full of traitors as if I had been
a tailor, just when the whole damn ball of yarn
had disappeared and I looked lost, just before
tea time, with an over to go I bowled them out.

# ODYSSEUS, ODD MAN OUT



My name is writ large.
I must survive in translation
fear not the symmetry of the sun
though melanoma is always a
possibility and separation:

I live life in quiet desperation
on the run like I'm in the witness
protection racket; I'm hamstrung
my balls are old and worn
I am caught in a net of my undoing.

# ODYSSEUS HAS A SEX CHANGE

Now that he has traded
in his aegis, time for a second look—
well-seasoned and commanding,
his hair like fishing nets is now spun
into black stockings.

Big hoop earrings of the kind
you could die for,
his muscular upper body frame
has now taken on a sports bra,
all dolled up in boots and lace.

It takes some getting used to
but sure, women can look strong
as Maud Gonne with a nose ring—
a force of nature forged into song,
a medallion on her war chest.

# ODYSSEUS' DEMISE AS A WRITER:
## ON THE SUMMER SOLSTICE

On the longest day and on and on
I will decompose myself, seeking
to bear witness to my shortcomings
becoming more compact, wallet thinner
not wasting the sunlight, not a crumb

carrying with me my little notebook
which I frequently fail to write in, but
I will overcome this by filling up the page
in front of your disbelieving eyes—
nose a sundial, fingers like spiders.

I will wear dark glasses to protect
my reputation, become anonymous
a shadow no longer than my thumb.
Going in and out of print, no one will
miss my coming out in paperback as
I disappear onto the remainder table.

# ODYSSEUS AT THE MALL

He is lost in the world
of American Eagle Outfitters
and Verizon Wireless,
looking for a hall of mirrors,
or a Hallmark card to send
to Penelope, and wonders
if she is a plus size woman
now, so he looks in the window
of "Torrid," sees a zebra stripe,
and thinks maybe a sheepskin.

How moccasins would soothe
his aching feet, perhaps a pedicure—
and like a 2nd hand Carnie he stands
next to a booth near Cinnabon.
What about a Zale's diamond?
But he decides instead to buy
a thermos of coffee with a mermaid
memento of his trip across
the Mediterranean and warm
enough to hold to his cold lips.

# ODYSSEUS AT REST



I sit in my seaweed chair,
looking out the window,
daydreaming about Circe,
my lost shipmates, the Cyclops.

Since I have slain the suitors
Penelope won't speak to me.
My loyal dog died of happiness.
Telemachus has gone to Rhodos.

While I deep in my cups
wish only for Lethe or Crete
I am no longer seasick
I drink crème-de-menthe.

My clothes tumble dry
in the sunlight, I long for
another journey. With my webbed
hands, I close this book.

# ODYSSEUS ON HIS DEATH BED

No bed of lettuce, no ambrosia blossom,
no sea change, or world of mermaids or mermen,
no make-believe, not again, no fires in
the belly, no padded cell, no hydra-headed
monster or Cyclops, no epigrams to write,
no loom to make and remake, a faithful
wife, a son traveling to Asia Minor.
Not even an afterlife worth waiting for.

## EPILOGUE:
## MY FATHER'S DRIFTWOOD

Once it had been a lamp.
My father drilled a hole,
ran a cord through it,
his offering of light,
shaped by his temper.
It balanced on one side
like a stork.

After he died, I took it apart,
kept the driftwood,
never bothered sanding it,
this wood made his icon.

When I left for England,
I took it to the beach,
left it on the sand
to be carried on a high tide.

Now I'm home again, finding
I don't fit the same as before.
I think of the man, unfinished
along this shore.
I wait for you to drift back.

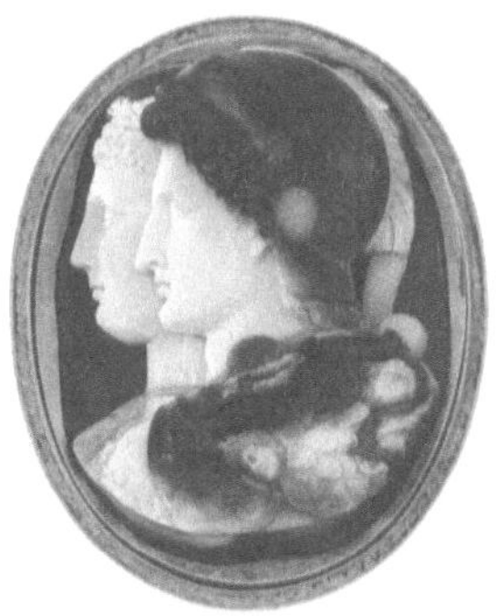

Adventure most unto itself
the soul condemned to be
attended by a single hound
its own identity.
        —Emily Dickinson

# II
# POETIC LANDSCAPES

# MASACCIO'S EXPULSION OF
ADAM AND EVE

*after the fresco by Masaccio, c. 1424-1427*

Sheltering her breast,
the first homeless woman
covers herself,

as Adam, hands over
his face, laments
what they have lost.

They drive themselves
forward without mercy,
children of the past.

Like figments out of Goya's
nightmares, out of chances,
too late to be forgiven.

No olive branch awaits—
the serpent left behind
still sways on its branch.

Dispelled into daylight
where an angel hangs above
them like a sword.

A rose-colored hell
unfolds their bodies, pink,
still unwrapped.

*IL VOLTO SANTO:*
## THE BLACK CHRIST OF LUCCA

His feet do not touch the ground,
the black Christ of Lucca,
arrived in Luni on an unmanned boat
from the Orient in the 8th century,
brought to Lucca by chariot
pulled by two untamed bulls.

May boats carry him above
the olive trees; even the marble
mountains of Carrara, Michelangelo's
bed, so light in color, but filled
with the weight of so much stone even
the Burghers of Calais couldn't escape.

*Il Volto Santo* carved by Nicodemus,
his eyes black as olives, wreathed
by angels who surround him, may
all the saints raise his spirit where
polished feet point to another glory
out of the groves of his black agony.

# WAITING FOR THE LAST SUPPER
# AT SANTA MARIA DELLA GRAZIE

We wait in line
for *The Last Supper*,
the man hawking jewelry
outside stops talking long
enough to say, *"20,000 lira."*

And the gypsy beggar
walks around with a cigarette
in his mouth, an open hand.
The bells are ringing in change,
but not for him.

Meanwhile, groups of tourists
pass, party of fifteen,
making another rotation, a rosary
as they turn the table over
once again before lunch.

We wait with the couple
from England, some Japanese,
a few Americans, an Italian film
star with her large dog
she lets everybody pet.

By noon, we haven't moved,
but a busload of Germans,
some French huddled in whispers,
even a soccer team goes past us,
still, Christ has not appeared.

Meanwhile in the church
a priest is taking confession,
our chances of being saved today
are nil; we wait in queue, hearts
beating without reservation.

# END OF AN ITALIAN SUMMER

At the sea wall
people write on the rock face
leaving their initials
near *Julia* on the beach.

A row of cabanas, barking dogs,
beach palms, and cactus,
spilling bougainvillea all
along the railroad tracks.

On the cliffs of Corneglia
we leave our friends,
the clocktower with its
Halloween face.

Orange and black with
whiskers for hours and minutes,
we have come to a perfect
resting place.

Like little sparrows,
*Il padrone* and his wife
are closing the window.
The father taking his boy

in hand, with school books,
to catch the next train
to Vernazza, where he will
learn to speak perfect English.

## SAN BERNARDINO

Tonight, the stars came down
like broken chords,
above San Bernardino on the hill,
the church bells in cadenzas.

Nearby, Ceccio's Restaurant
with its green awning and the
rings of Christmas tree lights near
our hotel, La Jaconda (*The Lantern*).

In the distance, Monterosso harbor,
brightest lamp of the northern star
guides us home to our room, after
wine and desert as we wave.

Across from us, a terraced hillside
glows with olive groves,
a phosphorescent sea and the sun
reflecting red like a grape.

Darkness grows with shadows
making patterns on this wall
of words, constellations swallow
us like children in our flowerbed.

# FIRENZE REMEMBERED



I remember leaving
  my sandals in Florence
    how I broke the strap
      footloose and tongue-loose.

I walked to the other
  side of the Arno to find
    a cobbler's shop, father and
      son, *padrone e figlio.*

Then, walked home barefoot
  to my pensione; days later
    I returned to claim my sole
      across the Ponte Vecchio.

## *PERSISTENCE OF MEMORY* BY DALI

Watches of memory are melting down,
the end of summertime has released
the hour to fall back on its chair.
White cabanas are closing along the beach.
*Il padrone* and his wife deep in the memory
of how the cobbled beach served as hope
for lobster backs, while the seconds
collected like flies on their faces.

Meanwhile, on the cliffs of memory
all is sunny on a different plane
where a buttery sky spreads evenly
into smoke from the mists hanging
above, no gulls to be seen on a canvas
stretching across untested landscape.

# CONTOURS

The Arno is its most beautiful between Pisa and Florence,
green and translucent, winding among amphitheaters of
    olive trees,
cypress silhouetted flat against the sky, cultivated hill
    towns of Tuscany,
the tile rooftops of Montelupo-Capraia, walls bleached
    white as laundry,
blooming from fields of sunflowers, nearby chevrons of
    fresh-cut hay.

Above, the slopes soften into olive groves, sun into
    shadow,
so power lines can hold sway, the Arno diminishing, but
    turning bluer
as it travels from Florence, the language growing richer,
    the smell
of earth and air stronger as we lean in towards Pisa at
    Empoli,
manure in the fields—the heat of an Italian summer in
    our nostrils.

Hillside forts appear like milestones, calling out the
    names of ancestors,
a single smokestack punctuates San Minato-Fucecchio,
    as we scream through Signa,
the embellishments of working-class Italians singing
    arias on the train,
speeding on their way to the *Torre Pendente*, leaning
    further, speaking
even more rapidly in exclamations, a crescendo of
    ear-splitting rails.

Cranes along the Arno stand along the banks waiting
     like question marks
for you to throw them a line, fish in the chalice of the
     river in no one's particular
time, nor, do I remember the meaning of night as seen
     from the train leaving
Florence, nor how I arrived in Pontadera from La Speiza,
     but instead how
the train station was made cool by the touch of marble
     from Carrara.

# CAMBIARE LA CASA

At night things move,
the floor creaks with the weight
of bones, a chair,
the solid bedstead slowly walks
across the ceiling, leg at a time.

Hooves of chair, an aria
like mountain goats, parade
the narrow paths and switchbacks
of interlocking grains, slow sides
of mountains of toilet paper, unwind,
mournful tuning of the dead.

All change positions as the
door jamb creaks, the walls
expand and contract according
to our breathing.

The release of windows,
untightening from their frames
to practice seeing not out, but in.
The Soul of every living and sleeping
room, now the dreams get up
to stir a little.

While the dead turn in their tight
little beds, the chest of drawers
opens to wrap thick arms
around our legs.
The whole town pulses,
ringing chimes echo with stories,
and stones, a pleasant
gentle hymn mixed in
with smoke from the candle.

The closet with its wardrobe
of sighs, hangers groaning with
their clothes, the tremor
of trembling curtains so full of sea
wondering at the night salt air.

Enfold. Shoes drop from above
rolling on their sides like cats
who change their fur so that when
we awake their markings disappear
like fire into smoke, the clouds
vanish into breezes, nothing seems
what it was awake,
candles turn to wax and flicker
the house can finally be laid to rest,
living things begin to breathe again
the groaning stops at last.

We echo
in this present tense.

# CURKARNA
*after the monoprint by Eva Pokorny, April 1991*

They are swimming in Matisse flavors,
all orange and red like coleslaw,
women with head scarves in a cafe
where gothic arches weave intersecting
patterns like they are part of a quilt,
grand design of a mosaic bazaar.

These girls and women with blue legs,
winnowing like tadpoles as they move among
the lime-green floating babies, heads
and arms translucent fins, faces, fish eyes,
glazing over sliced cakes, bowls of sugar cubes
and diamond-laced napkins, that spill

into the sinewy chairs with their backs
wrapping around them like eels, breasts
of fish bones, wisteria of clouds above,
growing into sea-green horses, a curtain
where they drown in soft shadows and curves,
the world which is a part of such women.

## CHINESE CHARACTER

I wrote in Chinese characters
and squiggles were feather fans
or sampans under a rosewood sun.
I learned the craft of robins, telling
songs to blinking generations,
legends of worms gone underground
and snows that never came in time
for spring, delicate as dragon wings.

Where are our family fortunes written,
what can a father tell his young?
Now there are wrinkles of crow's feet
drawn in around the eyes, red sunsets.
Only a portrait in sticks and fireflies,
a scratching down by pen-light
these signatures in line and ink,
Mandarin charm in an old man's wink.

# PATHOGENESIS

The ferry boats are made of white bone china,
sail in spirits across the water from Bremerton
past Alki and Duwamish Head, a drumbeat engine
thrumming in my head, safe port below silver clouds.
I sleep in my bed near Burlington Northern Railyard
rolled up in my blanket like a cigarette,
the world made visible in smoke and wind.
Vibrations sent along the line from another train's thunder.

Meanwhile, the feather of a gull
floats in the air above my skin, a girl on wings
calls my name, "*O Santa Fe,*"
your headlight burns a ring in my overcoat,
a leaf leaves color in the Autumn air,
yellow words mingle with red paper from the
vine maple, the scroll of a madrone's parchment,
and starlings scatter in the air like crosses.

"*Oh, Santa Fe*" the crow is cursing in the lines,
a cough comes from the throat of nearby woods
and robins nest in the masts of birches.
If I could find a way around this cold that thickens
like sugar in my blood, just for a cup of Joe
to hold against my chest, Oh Brother
would you spare some of your heart's wood
so I could live again, stir me with a breath?

Give voice to my fire, all along the ground
I hear my belly's rumblings, my ears
echo like tin cans, a wire is strung tight
for me to hear, but there are only lullabies
from the railbeds where long lost children

once lived; I wake to the ashes of dawn.
What I wouldn't give to rub my eyes and find
pennies someone had put there just for luck.

# WALKING PAPERS

Leaves rust on the hillside this fine afternoon,
the old railroad ties soaked black with creosote,
while oil drums are wearing new coats of paint,
and here in the yards it's lonesome for the whistle,
the gandy dancers are all gone, those rail-splitters
the seed men from Burlington Northern who laid
    fresh tracks.

No echoes of the pick axe to follow us home, only
a box car abandoned, that once made somebody's bed
where a man slept feet first so he wasn't crushed,
and the bottles rolled up and down all night long
while his head swelled with a lady's perfume.

Now you can't find a train to catch near Pier 86
where the fisher gulls skitter across the waterway.
They're unloading Datsuns from Japan that shine
in the night like sardine tins; the moss is green
as broken glass, and you can hear shouts of stevedores
down where trains used to hoot in the wilderness.

# GINGER AUTUMN

Ginger, peach, aplet-covered hills
with flecks of Autumn in your hair
crimson and yellow as vine maples.

Pigeons roost in the telephone wires
a slow freight moves like graffiti,
orange and rusted as a garter snake.

Blue and white cranes in the tideflats
a cast of forest green reflections
painted down to the waterline.

Metal plates of the Murray Morgan Bridge
shake to the tune of a logging truck
that lumbers across on its way home.

Boats rust away on their anchors,
the Bantry Bay Gig lies resting while I walk
these planks like a seasick sailor.

# VINCENZO

*Lessons from Our Elders*
*a series by Bill Turner*

El Greco painted him—
he led the charge against the Ottoman Turks
in the 1565 Siege of Malta.

Bearded, head dented like a helmet
you painted him in later years with a dog
in his lap, cross-eyed.

His hair had become autumnal,
you gave him a cigarette locked in his fist
like a smoking gun.

Who would have thought, after all
these years, murdered by two knights,
he'd still be around, fully armed?

In another painting he's gone to college
received his flat hat, baccalaureate
degree, he looked enlightened.

Full of the blazes in these paintings,
you paint him as Matisse with
the old master's spectacles looking on.

Vincenzo brought back to life, this man
of ambition all decked out, plotting
to smoke his next Lucky Strike perhaps?

# MARK THIS WALL

*an unsent letter from a Roman soldier, Hadrian's Wall*

I'm lonely here—
the places I didn't go
to defend this place
have given me a headache
for twenty years or so.

Its underpinnings in gorse
tiny flowers of thyme
grow through it, these stones
have bled more blood than men
and yet I'm full of hope.

The men it posted here
from Syria to Africa
who stood as sentry
through winter's outnumbered days
wish you were here.

      Love, Caia Flavius
       122 AD

# SHEEP GRAZING AT VINDOLANDA



Where Hadrian built his wall
a garrison of sheep are posted—
their heads blow in the evening
slow turning to watch the field.

As they graze, their simple selves
show such kind faces that even
an emperor would do an honor
bestowing upon them his gaze.

They love the grassy breezes
blowing back to them, so soft
they are and full of wool. They
barely speak while on patrol.

Content in their sheepish hearts
to roam along this frontier
and keep from straying
among the barbarians.

# FRATELLI'S COWS

In the beginning, the big makers
of ice cream spotted them round
and Rubenesque, big-bottomed cows
that mooed and swayed, full of romance.
Their udders were full as the moon,
their teats like bagpipes.

Fratelli's changed all that;
remember, cows were always cubist
care-givers of life.
Their milk is in a carton, isn't it?

Though the cows stood around a carousel
the field always had four corners
in their two-dimensional world,
the cows would unfold into twilight.

Cows with corners,
cows you could put in albums;
cows you could mail that would fit
into envelopes with sticky tongues.

In black and white,
these cows of film noir in angles
that bisected themselves; cows
you could fold into origami or make
paper airplanes with.

Cows spaced out,
patchwork, crazy-quilt cows that we see
on the sides of trucks and billboards,
flat as the landscape.

Cows to be painted in,
not by numbers, but the cow of Picasso
or Chagall, even Matisse, the fatted cow
waiting, just to be milked by you.
No one knows what's on their other side.

## THE SIXTH DAY OF THE CREATION
### woodcut, 1926, Escher

Comes man with pineapple trees,
Eve's arm slipping along his back,
hare and cat, the quilted fields.

Adam dark and hairy, Eve, blonde
dangerously intertwined, sleek
as Rodeo Drive, the hoary satyr

with his back turned, yet watching
cows-in-clover, palmetto umbrellas,
mango sunsets with a gathering storm.

Clouds all in view, the lost rat
ready to gnaw his way out, they look
at the creation as an afterthought.

In black and white, pillow-mattress-
ticking clouds will come, the furrows
of fields laid-out on a flat-screen television
to be followed by free-range children.

## SNAKES
### woodcut, 1969, Escher

In Escher's Gordian knot
the serpents are laid out
numbered like a compass rose
wrapped around itself
as seen from heaven above.

Tail to head to tail
on three-pronged sides
a smooth belly rises
like the sun with the flow
of just another day in Eden.

Meanwhile in the middle
of its interlocked cosmology
a galaxy waits to be born
that would not expel the fallen
where man and snake are one.

# FLAMIN' JUNE


*after the painting Flaming June*
*by Frederick Lord Leighton*

Flamin' June
sleeps in like a 'bludy' mushroom.
Bone-idle she is. "Oose she waitin' for
'er fancy man?" Asleep in crinoline.
'Ed on 'er bleedin' breast. Orange colour?
"O'll tell 'er anyway? More to life
than being a serviette." Wake up June! Oy!
"Oose she think she is, Queen of Mums?"
Dreamin', always dreamin'. Confess.
"June" I says, "Independence?
Yule never bludy get it because
you don' know 'ow to say No!
An' don' forget it!"

# VAN GOGH'S OPENING PITCH
*after the painting Sower with Setting Sun*

The blocked fields of color
wrapped with Autumn fences & haystacks
like shimmering fields of fans
with blue midline of sky
and the sower casting his seeds
          into the sunshine.

Van Gogh winds up!
As though delivering the first pitch
in brushstrokes, his face
a sun-burnt orange and the yellow
corn fields stand up to applaud
          doing the wave!

On the mound!
The big-boned right-hander
cranks, legs bent like a stork
for the follow through.
The sun's big as a sunflower
in the open field of harvest,
glowing fields of Dutch Iris
strike one. A fastball.

# SOLZHENITSYN AT THE BEACH
*Alexander Solzhenitsyn,*
*Nobel Prize Winner (1918-2008)*

I saw him yesterday,
balding, pot-belly, mutton chops
lantern jaw.
When he pulled his pants down
a moth flew out.
He was wearing his
swimming suit
with a red star.

I asked him about his
after life.
"I'm happy, I go swimming
twice a day."
I told him Putin invaded Georgia.
"Why Georgia, why not Florida?
That's where they are always
screwing up democracy!"

The last time I saw him
he was doing the Australian crawl
out beyond the ropes,
having a smoke,
practicing his dolphin kick,
leaving the buoys behind,
training for the 2022 Olympics.

# OYSTER LIGHT

They call it "oyster light,"
those Northwest painters.

On the half-shell
its luminous, iridescent self

where it opens to the
mother-of-pearl inside

its eyesight, the softness
full of illuminations

to contradict: a cataract,
a cloud of vision

calling up our ancestors
out of silver-gelatin past.

Photographs in a swirl
of our fingerprints.

HUDSON RIVER SCHOOL
LANDSCAPE PAINTERS
*"The old and picturesque will soon be*
*dismembered."*
              —Frederick Church


Through the arches and temples of Arcady
they are looking for the spirit above
Niagara Falls, or turning to John the Baptist
preaching in the wilderness of Colorado.
In Labrador an iceberg rises, Grand Manon Island
in the Bay of Fundy to Mt. Etna's burned-
out cone smoking as seen from Taormina.
The Rock of Gibraltar looks stranded as Ayres
Rock in Australia, ruins that remind us of Rome;
a plangent sunset in Florida that burns like
a filament in the mind, out of a Walter Scott novel;
vistas of the Campagna or Cuernavaca;
the Venetian School of water music on the Hudson
River of glass with Barbizon mists rising to the
ethereal
in North Carolina above a "fermenting slough," made
by Cole and Chambers, Church and Bierstadt.


Look outside, you'll see Mt. Rainier in blue,
the fiberglass cone of the glass kiln, the 19th Street
string suspension bridge, a mandolin, and Tacoma's
geodesic wooden dome like a Ukrainian Easter egg.
There is still a landscape here to be painted,
across the sky, evening in Arcady, implications
of paint, flecks in the eye washing to the shores
of Commencement Bay and beyond the Olympics
to Capri and Jamaican rum skies, a beach to quiet
the nerves, a valley out of Bierstadt that would

do credit to Ansel Adams; these Hudson River painters
with a vision made of canvas and wooden frames.
Sailing away on an idyllic tide, it is the world we
would
all want to see, untested by industrial slag, no zinc or
lead
to interfere with scenes that have never had a hard
life
as deer and eagles still untroubled by hunters
take shape out of the pigment of their imaginations.

# BELLA AND ME ON MT. RUSHMORE

Half in shadow, half in light
I hold her up in front of
Washington and Jefferson,
to the left of Abe Lincoln,
filling in the gap between
Teddy Roosevelt's spectacles
where she fits just right.

Perched on my shoulder
among Borglum's Presidents,
Bella smiles happily on cue
as I with my craggy face,
bad dental work, chipped tooth
fit in nicely and certainly am
not amiss among the rockfall.

# LITTLE CHAPEL IN WALL DRUGS, SOUTH DAKOTA

A rosette window and cross
above the altar.
*Tonka* pounding across
the wooden floors of the prairie.
I hear the Bison still—
pine ceiling with knotholes
too small to fit through for a sinner
but perfect for a red-headed woodpecker.

Yellow walls of bricks that cool
like buckskin, a wooden bench
to sit on while I'm resting, praying
relief from the heat of the leathery sun,
my heart beating its tom-tom.
I've come to feel some calm
for here—I don't feel so small.

# HUNTERS IN THE SNOW
### *after the painting by Bruegel*

Belgium is frozen over—
outside the gates of Antwerp
the hunters are remorseless
dogs with tails like scythes
carve a leaden landscape.

Geese make iron crosses
in the low, offending sky.
Below, children are skating
making circles on the ice
hoping the sun will come back.

The Protestants are hunted
and the humanists haunted
by red emblazoned cardinals
who burn the cities and hang
the heads of scholars high.

Mercator is in Rupelmonde prison,
using Gemma's triangulation
to find a way out, until finally
the door opens and he emerges
into the spring of Flemish fields.

Mercator is lying low,
working on his globes, plotting a horizon
line that will join the earth—
both Protestant and Catholic—
a map to make the world whole.

## REMEMBERED LIGHT

*from an exhibit of glass fragments from World War II.*
*Shards were collected by Frederick Alexander*
*McDonald, chaplain.*
*Each fragment, part of a larger piece, told its own story*
*from the broken cities of the world.*
    —Tacoma Art Museum, Tacoma, Washington

Some cathedrals still stand, ornate and Gothic
medieval, some rebuilt on the ground where
they were destroyed.

The remains of Charlemagne's bones hidden
in the woods returned to Aachen where they still
rest as a shrine.

  A woman like a holy ghost fleeing down a road
  carries two black suitcases in her haste.
  Nearby, a wrecked train.

  A mother in Wiesbaden whose child
  blown from her arms was never
  seen again.

In Verdun, light murdered the street,
a "shattered synagogue" used for bombing practice
while nearby, a choir rehearsed.

  In Cologne, "only the cathedral survived"
  the British bombs where the Rose window
  had been removed.

  Nothing bloomed there but white sheets
  in the windows waving for the dead
  to make their shrouds.

In Frankfurter Dom, the scalp of St. Bartholomew
pulled from a drawer with yellowish-grayish hair
where emperors were once anointed.

> Last of all my namesake, St. Michael's in
> Coventry,
> first target of the Luftwaffe, rebuilt and
> rising
> into a new orbit of light.

# CHESTERFIELD-ST. MARY, WELL DRESSING

keeps watch over the vestry,
the sarcophagi, carved oak
and the deep red stained glass,
dark walls of timbers enclose us.

This high church ceremony
where we bow our heads
before the station of the cross,
the baptismal fount, where a baby
is dipped, anointed with holy words
like chocolate.

A bell rings, the red light is on,
bread is being consecrated, ladies
in broad flowering hats, men in dark suits
stand in line, a life is given, not
to be taken away. The clay is still wet.

Faces of egg shells, nuts, holly berries,
wheat crescents, a sky made of hydrangeas,
small cones and dry leaves mark a cross.
We are spared a plague this day on all
our houses when a child is born.

# ST. NICHOLAS OF TURKEY

Patron saint of clerics, sailors, children, animals
and lost women who came from Patara, his life was
    exemplary.

Saved three boys who were butchered for ham and
    reassembled
their body parts; that is why he's a friend of clerics.

Saved three prostitutes who were being sold by their
    father
using money from their dowry, converting them to nuns.

Saved a sailor who was lost at sea, whose soul he kept
    afloat
and became a friend to seamen.

Was buried, entombed in Bari where the myrrh from
his body attracted people from all over just to smell
the sweetness of his soul.

BOUQUET

This could be a mirage: these fields of Dutch Iris
blue as the Cote d'Azur, the waves tended by women
in broad-brimmed hats, dipping into the paddies
like coolie laborers, their legs bending like straws.

A Steller's jay hops along the road delivering a chanson
to the razzing crows, the iris blooming in bundles,
hand-picked cold ribbons that wave as you pass beyond
into what could be fields of Holland or France.

The farms divide into Skagit Valley flatlands, bands
of tulips whose colors rest in the eyes' pure palette,
distillations of hues, shimmering in pools that form
lakes on the frozen highway even while you watch.

Blink: the image moves to pass, leaving dry pavement
where it stood, the rear-view mirror returns to empty
as you travel onto the cloverleaf above your head—
where automobiles bright as ornamental poppies flash.

# TWO VIEWS OF BATH

I  Wake at Bath

A medusa skull of snake limbs,
the crab apple struck dead, its side split
by lightning lies among burnt timbers
near Napoleon's vases given to Josephine,
a row of copper beeches serpentine
along a drive near the Royal Crescent.

There's murder in this English weather—
cracks of thunder like cannonballs
signal my surrender, crouched in hiding
among the Botanical Gardens, bullets of hail
where it cuts at my windpipe.

Slings and arrows of rain
sting like a pen knife beneath the collar
from an Agatha Christie novel.
The fountain is spouting the wounds
of dying Romans, or a doomed emperor,

or a traveler set on escaping—
not emperor or royalty, or disloyal subject—
but cold and waiting for an opening
to execute a retreat, or fake sanctuary
always mindful of cold feet.

II   Sydney Gardens

Sydney Gardens, a quiet simple ground
with a leaning picket fence while I cross
the bridge above the Great Western Rail
looking down to the Kennet-Avon Canal,
so calm you forget it flows. I make the turn
up Sham Castle Lane, a road narrowing to a path
through private grounds where you can see
across the valley's bowl to the Royal Crescent,
the Georgian architecture of Bath, now moving
up Henrietta Street in increments, arranged
in orderly rows where the trail ends in footsteps,
toward dinner hour at six o'clock my pen
casts its shadow like a sundial.

# ON THE ROAD TO STEILACOOM
### *for Daniella, Eleana, and Jean*

Winding down to the creek beneath
a natural canopy of trees, maples
on each side, we come to the estuary
filling up Chamber's Creek and see
the sand bars where teens wade out in
the middle of July with their paddle boards
skinny-dipping with their friends.
The shallows like unplayable lies.

But we drive on toward Steilacoom
along the water near the rail line,
a bridge crossing and sign, then pull
off the road to find a deer staring at us
in shadow among the blackberry bushes
and alder trees, nibbling on the leaves,
her ears following us like radar, but
friendly enough, forgiving as we take up
her parking space.

We're only here for a minute or two
trying to escape the chicane
of cars weaving by the hillside. To escape
the drivers, we shelter like the deer
they never see, invisible to them,
and are protected by the hillside
where no one can reach us, as we
wait for the road to clear before pulling
out, the deer still drinking in the shade.

# AT CHIEF SEALTH'S GRAVE, SUQUAMISH

For us his mound is most sacred,
among the unknown graves, Qual-Qual Blue,
a man of 108 years and Kil-She-Bet-Sut.
For him they made a longhouse from canoes,
blackened with pitch and beneath it are strewn
tributes of pine cones, boughs, clamshells,
feathers, beadwork, the paper-thin money plant,
Chinese lanterns, ribbons, foil and bark,
all blessings of past and present are due.

Looking across the Sound toward Seattle,
all that is vested in earth faces water.
Having come on ferry and by foot to this, his
burial mound. Sun-through-the-firs, peace-among-
all-brothers, love-for-the-trusted word he gave.
We come here to touch a place of bleeding hearts
where looking from a knoll, above the mission roof
there are glimpses of the Cascades, and across
the water it is written in wakes, where the spirit
lives, people gaze across at you without knowing.
You are the name that gave them their names.

# THE LONG ROOM AT TRINITY COLLEGE

To walk under the arched ceiling, row upon row
of gold-bound books, the white busts of poets,
clergymen and scholars to the end and never
hear a voice above a cough or whisper,
only the squeak of shoe leather intrudes
while people gather around the *Book of Kells*
anxious to have their own illuminations.

And then to move among relics of writers,
Russell, Joyce and Wilde makes one a child.
Yeats' half-mile trophy, Synge's typewriter and camera,
and the Otway harp framed there in the corner.
It makes me mute as though I'd entered church,
keeping quiet as a candle, content to see the light
passed on from another man's altar.

# III
# PERSONAES

# THE VENTRILOQUIST

I have learned to throw it
up the stairs and around corners
so that it comes back to me
like wind down a blind alley.
I can place it in the air,
among telephone wires,
or within the cries of gulls,
letting it roar like thunder
or funnel it underground
in the digging of moles,
the slow shifting of rocks,
roots holding their breath.

How many parts can it take?
How many mouths must I feed?
Dogs bark in my angry voice,
cats scream beneath my window,
even the crows mock me.
At night when I try to sleep
it sings to me an old lullaby
from the cradle of my throat:
I ask, "Who is the wooden one
sounding out these words,
which the master, the dummy?"
Whose lips are moving now?

# THE MAN WHO BROKE INTO SONG

His tongue had been dead a long, fallow time,
speech was a ragged saw, or a step-ladder,
or a fence to keep prowling strangers out;
words were labor now, he split no stones.
He spent his youth sweating with a dream,
toiling in the kitchen with a grammar.
What did he need with words? Every night
he dreamed of giving up his plot of bones.

Now was he to cut his baby teeth again,
go back to rocking in an easy chair,
pick up the shovel and the rusty plow?
Let them take those books and fill a barn,
or spread them over the pasture like manure
or teach a stone-deaf farmer how to crow.

# WALT WHITMAN, LEAVES OF
# GRASS BLOWERS
*from a postcard sent by Allen Braden*

The poet stands his ground
carrying a grass blower.
Having cleared the garden path
he looks across the field,
wearing his broad Bolivar hat,
now gestures as if to say: *Well done.*

What to clear next? The thorns
of thought, or edge along his unruly prose?
Will it be Clematis, English Ivy or Morning
Glory, the detritus of what chokes us or
only annoying dandy lions?

What can he do but fill in the field of
his verses and begin again, get back to work
on digging a hole for refuse, make a compost heap
from all the leaves and branches, mulch the soil
so the world becomes democratic and out
of the sum remainder glean new clippings
to plant in the sun.

# I SAW WALT WHITMAN IN WRIGHT PARK

proselytizing to the crows who were
ranting back. He threw some bread crumbs
on the pond and said:
"Here, this is for humanity.
I keep it along with my freezer jam
We have so little to eat."

His one good ear was tuned
in to the robins and with his ear trumpet
he expounded on the Song of Man,
although his words rang hollow
to the Flicker, who was tapping out his
Morse Code above the car alarms.

His claims of sovereignty
over the earth fell on the deaf ears
of the moles who were busy kicking
up dirt and the squirrels seemed largely
to ignore him, sniffing out nuts and running
back and forth like demented poets.

When I left I could still hear his
cries of brotherhood for ants, as the dragonflies
buzzed around the crown of his white hair—
like a halo above a swamp fire. "All grass
clippings are the same!" I heard him say.

And as the police hauled him away
with his piece of cardboard and sleeping bag,
still feeding the pigeons, he screamed to beast and fowl:
"A park is a Democracy!"—which got the attention
of the geese, who honked profusely with thanks!

# THE SNOWMAN SPEAKS
### *To Wallace Stevens*

In the park nothing is moving,
but footprints leaving
fresh tracks. Nothing is happening,
nothing far, nothing near.

And the trees are shivering
in memory of their leaves
and I am here writing it all down
with my carrot nose.

And where are the owls
in the trees, the family of raccoons
that watch me from behind
their masks? Nothing from without.

The nothing that is here—
and the nothing that is not here.
Only the snowman knows, only
the snowman who has no clothes.

# PROUST IN THE PARK

Making my rounds, I saw him today
puffing on his pipe, tie pin
secure and talking to the squirrels
as if he owned the place.

His shoes were brightly polished
and if I looked there I could see
his face, intelligent, aristocratic,
his hands delicate, his moustache

neatly brushed, top-buttoned overcoat
stiff collar, wearing a bowler hat.
He seemed to be memorizing
the names of the trees: Red Oak,

Cypress, Norway Maple, Caucasian
Ash and his favorite, the Paper
Birch. He stripped off the bark and
began to write, noting the sky.

Light askance, he cataloged
every bird: The Purple Thrush,
Chickadee, and Lark, what a figure
he cut—so debonair—his patent

leather hair in place—I thought:
this must be his day off away
from the gossip of women and men
with their tiresome self-importance.

Observing the corrugated pond:
Lord and Lady Mallard, the Shovellers
turning in tight circles like society
divas and debutantes.

How each Cedar Waxwing passes
along a berry to the next until they're fed,
like a cocktail party where everyone
demurely leaves their olive to the last.

How much to find in nature, what it
says about the man—how he must
return and dip his Madeleine in tea
and watch it melt away like pretense.

He passed the time looking at
his watch as though every minute
counted: past, present and future
time rolled into one tense.

# A PARK IS A CATHEDRAL

A park is a cathedral
the red oaks are the walls,
with stained-glass leaves
the path between, a transept.

And in the nave—
the altar where we pray
for peace and quiet
above the gibbering,

above, the gibbous moon,
a holy wafer to place
beneath the tongue
receiving the Eucharist.

The fountain is where
we purge ourselves—
our sins made manifest
within the healing range of crows.

Crosswords left behind,
candy wrappers,
aluminum cans, plastic
for the recyclables.

Park benches are the pews,
where we kneel before
the squirrels to offer crumbs
on what to them is holy ground.

Whatever confessions we
make to ourselves
are in whispers, like cedar waxwings
where the cedar boughs.

# A SENSITIVE PLANT

Touch the leaves, ask them
if they're sensitive. Do they know
a predator from a friend?

Tell them you mean no harm—
you, who only want to
ask them as they fold shut

like a letter in the envelope
of your hand, closing at your
own singular touch.

Run your finger along the spine
then ask them what they want—
some reassurance of light?

Say you're only browsing
in the conservatory of life,
have no power over them.

That you a sensitive human
too would never harm them
just to satisfy your curiosity.

Tell them that when we touch
for the joy of ever-giving life
we are all sensitive plants!

# MARY, MARY AND JACK THE LAD

Are your buds bursting
from the trees like robins or roses
from a vase in Florentine ways,
swelling into candle holders
like William Morris' *Art Nouveau*?

How does your garden grow?
Is it filled with juicy snails,
are there slugs-a-plenty
ready to strip your leafy greens,
do your toes make curlicues like Buddleia?

Are your lips like Rhododendrons,
do arms flower into crabapple and cherry?
Do you fill them with beauty bark
or Spanish moss among the cockleshells
of your virginal heart?

Do you have a Tibetan bell to sound?
Are your breasts red as pomegranates?
Do you catch the sun's full glory
ripe as an apple on your neck or
do you have a hidden trellis?

Come, climb up my towery vine,
your dowry is in your shoe.
Will your fertile fields of charms
give up their fruit or will you bear
all of me in your willowy arms?

Just to be your willing gardener
I would prune away each suitor;
I would put down my clippers, find
a place for us to nip into just
for the pleasure of your elixir.

# RAPUNZEL

Lets her hair down to the floorboard,
hangs up stars in the rear-view mirror
while the boys are out playing cards,
sporting with their flashy cars.

*Let down your hair, Rapunzel,*
let him climb into your heart
but don't expect him to help
you buckle your seat belt.

*Let down your hair, Rapunzel,*
find another road to go,
floating across the center line,
the prince asleep at the wheel,
listening to the radio.

*Let down your hair, Rapunzel,*
let him keep his fast hands to himself.
*Let down your hair, Rapunzel,*
but keep the key to all those
beautiful golden locks.

# HOW CARRIE HOWARD'S DAUGHTER
# LEARNED TO LOVE 'DA' MOON

You no longer need to tremble in fear
my daughter, you turned away the first time.
Was it fear, something left undone?

You only squirmed and would not look
at its round Mao face. Did it remind you
of your orphanage in China, the milk
you never drank, down the silk road
of your umbilical cord?

I could understand such fear.
I was lost before you, without son
or daughter, it was only later I realized
how sad the moon made your face,
a side you didn't know.

Now you thrill to its charms
and one night when I took you out
to see (the night was clear),
you said in your baby-Bronx accent:

*"Hey, moon, you want a bottle?"*
It was only then I could agree:
what had been half-empty became full,
the moon pouring out its poetry.

# HARRY POTTER AND THE DAWN EXPRESS

Two blue moon phone boxes stand
side by side like policemen
attracting the sun's gold badge,
the new moon surrendering itself
fades now, while the red-eye
express is still dawning.

The whistle goes like a tea kettle.
Harry finds himself far from
the sweeper's broom, the closet door.
Suddenly he finds his compartment
out of nowhere, sees his face
in the window, ready to appear.

The conductor waves his wand,
in between platforms 9 and 10
the scene begins to roll again.
As the rails begin to widen, our boy
Potter looks on, glasses taped together
as if struck by lightning into song.

In the deep Parrish-blue sky
of morning, the robin leaves
its trill in rose window certainty.
No one has risen yet but the call
of a diesel engine gives birth
to a train sounding its English horn,

Rumbling as it comes soft
to the station where pine boughs
still hold winter nests in shallow day.
Our Harry practices his wizard turns
beyond his fledgling vanishing point, darts
like a Snitch into the wind's curve.

# GOODBYE TO HOGWARTS

*Don't let the Muggles grind you down.*

The circle on the square
the synthetic turf where
we played chess with men
as large as the ones on Apu Nui.

The art deco compass Rose
and the flag flying upside down
Lion's breath—we'll miss you all:
Misses, Mrs. and Misters,
and all our little friends at school.

Flying owls and squirrels,
cats that go splat! One-eyed
newts and salamanders to remind
us of the tasty gruel served up
in the great banquet hall.

The Dumbledores who made
us proud, the eely executioners
like Snape, scouts, cooks, giants
and tadpoles that we lived with.

From now on it's a muggle's world
we have to live in, the map
made flat in its 2-dimensions
with very little magic—but
lots of everyday commonplaces.

No walls to come alive with faces
or two-footed floors that gave
way to slippery slides, no spells to
cast no magic wands or broomsticks
that jump out of the corners.

Just i-macs, apples and i-pods,
smart phones (how smart is that?),
the electronic hoodwinks of an
artificial world with no intelligence
to keep from falling out of trees.

# ELEGY FOR ARIEL

*Any time not spent on the wire is marking time.*
                                        —Karl Wallenda

Star-crossed, only a fixed pole to guide him,
he began his walk, and when the wind began to gust,
he shook, lowering his pole, kneeling, obedient
to the hairline, a fracture that divided breath,
heaven from earth, he tried to right the balance
swinging against him in ever-widening strokes.

Then a memory of falling, angels and men, the
     pyramid
of his family that tumbled in Detroit, not counting
all the history of walks on wires, stretching out
like moonbeams into space; he sank down slowly
to his knees, trying to grasp the wire spinning
through his hands, the slipping away of his lifeline.

His friends called; what name could hold him now?
He missed the thread, still clutching his pole,
could he cheat gravity to span the gaping air—*no*.
Now his life in half-lives shrinking smaller,
curling towards his body hurtling past his heels,
waiting for the slap of sidewalk to deliver him.

# VENUS IN THE ANTIQUE MALL

An eggshell over one breast
a starfish on the other
she rises like Aphrodite from the foam
of Uranus's castration
a new woman: fillets for ribs
sitting in a white bird bath
surrounded by driftwood and moss.

Her bust tilted like the prow of a ship
though in drydock, now she hopes
for a tide to lift her like a sea anemone—
perhaps she'll open on a clamshell
a parasol to shade her eyes,
red from rubbing her tears into salt,
finished as a masthead in her afterlife.

# GRACE NOTES

Outside the leaves are falling
in their sweet harmonies
of green and gold,
the maples are shedding
their grace notes
and the rain is steady
keeping time with its brushes
like a ballad.

There is space between notes
and the hope of the bass player
that he gets his solo in
may go unnoticed,
but deep in the throat
of the vocalist, a bird begins
its melody, a trill
you haven't heard before:
a love that no one sees.

# VOLARE' 1958

California trailer parks, on vacation,
freedom of camping by the riverbank;
a pool to swim in, the summer ahead,
the sky an anthem I could sing from.
Opening the windows of our Buick Special
crossing at the California border,
ready for the fruit and vegetable check,
the road emptying to Redding motels.

The whole wide Pacific Ocean lies ahead,
running on the beach, snapping towels,
ear to the ground for clams,
girls posing on racks of driftwood,
mermaids with tails and Domenico Modugno
singing his flying song while I
try to keep my hair combed.

Burning in the sun, breezy as palms
and cocoa oil; I cover every pore
lie awake listening to Mr. Acker Bilk
and hum "The Stranger on the Shore,"
the vibrato of his clarinet coming from
the bell of my throat while a silhouette
calls me back to another shape-shifter.

A girl is waiting in her swimsuit
in a theatre; I would hold her there,
slink my arm around the back of her seat.
I sleep for two in my overcrowded bed
with thoughts of loves who abandoned me,
and I am already dreaming of another
who I can only imagine on a shiny cover.

I have memorized her license plate and phone number.
There are children growing in the garden
like hydrangeas with curly heads,
the wind has promised me a place
to live "Beyond the Sea" of Bobby Darin,
where my future goes round in vinyl
just waiting like a new 45 to drop
from the spindle onto the turntable.

# SAMBA SENTIMENTAL

Coffee is thrumming in my head.
I am my broad-brimmed self, half-Panama
sitting in the window, looking for the lady
who is soulmate to my pulse.

O, for the warm rain
that will fill my palms
like banana leaves, soak my rubbery skin,
let me sing to open-fretted girls
shaped like guitars.

We're all children of the dance
floating on the tide table
of romance. Touch my tickling feet.
Come, rub your sand between my toes.
Make love with your sexy elbows.

# THE POPE FROM IPANEMA

Short and tan and full of promise
the Pope from Ipanema goes walking
and as he crosses each one he blesses
                                    *goes "Ahhh."*

When he walks it's like a homily
that almost takes your holy breath away
and as he crosses each one he blesses
                                    *goes "Ahhh."*

O, but he crosses so slowly,
how can I tell him I love him?
But each day at the Holy See
He goes straight to it—not to me.

Short and tan and full of promise
the Pope from Ipanema goes walking
and as he crosses each one he blesses
                                    *goes "Ahhh."*

O, but my skin is like sugar,
how can I tell him I'm not vinegar?
But each day at the Holy See
He goes straight to it—not to me.

When he walks, he carries condoms
that move so gently, and sway so softly
that when he passes, each one he passes
                                    *goes "Ahhh."*

When he goes to Sugar Loaf mountain
He takes his time with the Holy Virgin,
And when he crosses each one he blesses
                    *goes "Ahhh."*

O, but I watch him so sadly,
how can I tell him I'm pregnant?
But each day at the Holy See,
He looks straight at it—not at me.

Tall and tan, and dark and handsome,
the Pope from Ipanema goes prancing,
but he just doesn't see. No, he just doesn't see.

## MUSIC OF THE PARIS CONSERVATORY
## SUNDAY CONCERT

From the harshness of a cold,
rainy Sunday afternoon
the winds reverberate
in sounds of daffodils—
clarinet and oboe, horn
and bassoon.

Hear the alto sax's
rich melody, the saxophone
a kind of daffodil that
warbles on the reed's tongue,
arpeggios play up and down
the stem.

A gold-throated voice rising
from its bell, deep rondos
a la Turk, a la Paul Desmond
larks filling the air, a nocturne
that shimmers in blues, greens
like a pear.

A short, fat little French horn
player huffs and puffs,
the clarinetist tall and green
as a pine, the pianist a slender
willow, the wind I hear is holding
court outside.

# SWAN UPPING

I think you are a swan at times,
beautiful long neck, straight white precious teeth.
You swim around me in great circles
showing off your power glide, falling in love
with your own reflection, below the surface,
working so hard just to stay afloat
while I counterweight your tiny feet,
to catch you as my holy ghost and poet.

I come to your bed a bit bedraggled
dreaming of counting you as my own,
leaving my signature, a maker's mark,
but I'm no one to take you with my charm,
so it is my joy to watch you float away
under this spell I count as human.

# SUMMER TRIANGLE

Last night I saw a swan in flight
in Deneb from Winter's Northern Cross,
heard music from the lyre marked by Vega,
Orpheus played across the spheres
with showers of the Milky Way.

Altair, the Eagle, kept watch
from the third side, one eye always open
circling above. I have torn a page
from the book of my writer's spine,
a leaf to design this summer triangle on.

At 10 o'clock I find it at the Zenith;
through all of August it guides my way,
frames the night, while down the street
a cue ball breaks and scatters the field—
as I rerack these same stars every night

# A WINTER SKY
*"There will be Stars"*
        —Jean Musser

Sometime tonight there will be stars.
And a moon that leaves its imprint
like a sestina, in a cocktail hour sky
full of the Milky Way spilling its clotted cream
onto the vertiginous dark, leaving our heads
spinning a dime-a-dance while we try to sleep,
but finding our dreams awake us, so instead
we go out into the carousel night where
everything's as certain as Saturn's rings
or winter's delight, the Northern Cross
has us in it its sights.

You can be sure there will be stars enough
to count, an occasional satellite blinking
its blessing along its icy path disappearing
on the other side of the rear-view mirror
far beyond the sun, and yes there will be
dancing among the stars tonight, underneath
the great glitter ball of the universe. Come!

# TO MY BOATHOUSE AT LAUGHARNE, DYLAN THOMAS

One last time from the shed
          I look down to see
the estuary and St. John's Hill
          knowing my tide's gone out.
I won't be coming home—
          but in my ears a shell—
I'll carry this tune—the sound
          of my words like stones.

## LAST CALL

The dolphins would be walking to shore
and I would be watching poised
on the cliffs above New Quay,
where only a spouting rock
throws up its periscope of spray.
There is nothing on the horizon
and I am breathing softly as a pigeon
as though I would frighten them away.

In hopes, my eyes are widening
as though my will would make them
leap headlong in furrows,
sprinting over the waves like gales.
But the only bottle-noses that I see
are men leaving the pubs,
whistling and burbling to each other
mouths wet, full of foam, and they are
singing to each other like Wales.

# A WORD FROM ROETHKE

I poise against the light
on this cold day,
the brightness in my head
being clear-edged enough
to sharpen my lead.
Leaves break me.

The cold snapping back
this pen against dullness.
Chill words for a chill day.
No diatribe, a quiet rant.
How else can I feel what
rubs against me?

# PORTWAY TAVERN, ON THE COLUMBIA

At the buddy's bar where
we bend our elbows, wood
worn smooth from glasses
rubbing against seamen's arms,

we fly under the pirate's flag
of a half-mast hangover where
men were shanghaied—dropped
into a boat through a trap door.

And men traded blows
like 2 x 4's in the Fightin'
Pit below the upright piano
where Bill played songs for Lila.

Last stop out of Astoria
for the master mariners,
the lumber crews who drank
their fill of lager-heads.

A belt hangs from the wall—
the "Whippersnapper" as the girls
waited upstairs for men
to stumble on their sea legs.

Jenny brings us two beers,
Joe goes back to work. This
would be a good place for
the tsunami to hit. Lots of waffle fries

to ride out the waves beating
on the piers, adrift on a life
raft, plugging the holes with
Tillamook cheeseburgers.

## THE GIANTS OF ASTORIA

Here they enter along
the waterfront, travelling on ships
to the underground sewers and
culverts, bringing their culture
of disease. No space is too
small for them, the rule of thumb
is what they use, a little like the
"Glory Hand" of Whitby where
a light in the window meant thieves
could enter the house. Here they
are the "uninvited," leaving their footprints
without an afterthought, as workers
bait the manholes, run for cover.
No rat is too large for Astoria.
There will always be a home for them
here at the mouth of the Columbia.

# COMPOST HEAP



I've grappled long enough
trying to nurture plants,
milking the ice box,
keeping the fire alive
and my own belly quiet.

No more rats of the mind
that gnaw on sleep
with straw and chicken wire,
working back towards scratch,
I dream of compost heaps.

A place to pile the dearth
of leaves, potato skins and coffee
grounds enough for a divorce.
Regarding all vegetable matters,
let the leftovers take their course.

## PONDLIFE

Today in the swamp I saw
two hooded mergansers going
round and round in a tango
stretching their necks out of water
rising like plumes of smoke
before they settled back.

Every limb was dripping,
the spongy ground sucked at my feet
and the pond had compounded
its banks rising over the rotting stumps
seemed to be floating until roots
and trees rose out of the debris.

I waited for the path to disappear
in front of me as if I was in
a science fiction movie, the surreal
surrendered to me in a scene only
I could rescue before it claimed
me as a witness.

Later I was found after the pond
went back to being a pond again.
I became a story where I had walked
in life. I left only a set of footprints.
They discovered me in a tree after
the water subsided, my arms a semaphore.

I made a splash for one day in the local
news, until once again I returned to earth,
became an obituary for someone

to walk over, returned back to the soil
where I came from, reborn in the suck
of an afterlife.

# A DIRGE FOR ALISA DIMITRIJEVA



*Dirty men cover me*
*with their weeds*
*and where I lie*
*the ground's all*
*eaten up with worms.*

*But I was not guilty,*
*just a teen-age girl*
*who asked a stranger*
*for a ride, now I'm gossip.*

*I got into a stranger's car;*
*they found me Boxing Day*
*all unwrapped, delivered*
*on the Queen's Estate.*

*They say I've been here months,*
*days don't count, so many*
*people must have walked by*
*me now come to look.*

*"It must have been a midnight*
*job," someone said. "We live on*
*a canal and dead bodies are*
*always being thrown into the water,"*

*said Mrs. Swallow. "This is a much
nicer resting place, especially
after such a violent crime." And
I agree. It's peaceful here.*

# TAKE TIME TO STEAL THE LILACS
*for Jim and Jacqueline Colburn*

They're free and fragrant
and sometimes even flagrant
for their touch may rub off
on your fingers, each to each
you may gather so they
fill your arms, hold them close.
Your breath will be transformed
and you will flourish among
the uninformed, not so much
famous as newly scented
and warm and very arrested.

# AS THOUGH I WAS PROUST TAKING MY EVENING STROLL

*But alas, I was alone and I felt as if I was*
*setting out to pay a neighborhood visit like*
*those that Swann used to pay us after dinner.*
*—Remembrance of Things Past*

I went outside and there were
crystals on the pavement
and the air was spun from lace,
the trees were candelabras
and on each limb a lighted candle.
There were many moons to watch
and a picture in each window
but no face!

There was no Gilberte or Albertine
to meet, no Duchess of Guermantes
in sight in our neighborhood, not where
I lived far from the Faubourg St. Germain
and the only party wasn't the salon of
Madame Verdurin or even Odette Swann
but a raucous left-over beer and garden party
in a tent.

I wandered over the lawn, floating
across the streets of darkness.
Corridors of apple trees parted before me.
Jupiter was blazing and Orion's Belt
had turned. Jean, I am here to remind
you not to forget who you are and to
remember who I am so we still live on
in our familiar names.

# LOVE'S A BLUR

Your hand spreads against
my shoulder, your eyes close
and seem to see what's behind me
while my back is turned.

We seem to be dancing
in freeze-frame,
held there, yet we turn
on our single pedestal.

Your wedding ring with
its triple garnets turns
like Orion's belt, pointing
toward my Taurus.

We are fixed there—
out of focus, certain
we are not alone, because
so much love surrounds us.

# CHAGALL DREAMS

He is carrying his beloved Bella
above the village green, tilting
her sideways like the prow of a ship,
while he paints with the hooves
of a cow. Using the chimney steeple
as his nib, he writes down the hour.

A fish with wings flies by,
violins play with their own bows,
a pendulum clock is swinging above
the sun with the aura of a candle.
O, if you could hold it, encircling it all;
it's a world you could put your arms around.

A gouache of never-ending sky,
sea urchins in trills, rising into the ether
where women grow like Russian nesting dolls
and roosters crow to their glowing wives,
while everyone sings to the windmill of nature
in notes only a poet or a lover could decipher.

## PUTTING PROUST TO BED

I put Proust down in my chair.
His black hair, mischievous smile
and little pince-nez glasses
are at rest for the night, but
what will I dream of? Drinking
tea with Madeleines or strawberries
on my cornflakes, or the touch of
the back of his polished chair?
Or perhaps the crack in the Venetian
blinds? So much to remember as
the light filters through my room
from the moon. I only want to rest
my head on the floral design of
the pillow and live in the Belle Epoch
with beautiful people in attendance.

Yet, here I am in Tacoma, with smokestacks,
sand bars of the Puyallup River,
and the diesel horn from the Coast Starlight
coming in from the south—O to melt in
the roof of my mouth with Madeleines
would be delicious steeped in tea—
I want to believe in memory and all
that it brings—but I'm too drowsy by now,
so I turn in my covers of conversation
with myself, ready to accompany the rain
to sleep, hear the backwash of cars
outside to the steady tick of the clock
moving with its insect hands, and in my
cork-lined dreams I dream of Marcel Proust.

## WILLA CATHER

In her dark feathered hat
she stands out in her velvet coat,
a braided lanyard hangs
around her neck, eyes bright
as jet. A cameo choker
solid as the Midwest gleam
of the Great Plains in her face
casting a shadow as she rests
in the prairie cradle
of a chair, compass point in focus,
she measures you like
a theodolite checking out
the landscape.

# GIRL WITH THE PEARL EARRING

The light was her judgement
as she looked expectantly
toward her master, ear lobes still swollen
from the piercing she suffered,
but she was young and would heal.

When he saw her head turned toward him
that day in the window in Delft, illuminated
by light, he knew he must have her.
"Don't move," he said—then it was over
he remembered and so did she—

until her "cameo" role came: one evening
at dusk in October a moon appeared
lovely and growing in the shape
they would always know, hanging in
the lobe of the sky, a pearl earring.

ON MY LITTLE STREET OF DELFT

Outside my window
the little street of Delft
in horizontal boxes,
houses arranged as coffins,
a passport of myself
looking out the window
of the frame as though I'm
a rabbit, about to be shot.

Waiting for the sky to turn
that pale blue with clouds—
like the view of Delft
to Vermeer who never travelled
farther than a few square miles,
who lived within the confines
of his easel, and painted
what was about to happen

in his daily life, happy to see
the trees on his little street—
while I see shadows this morning,
a somber sunrise without a wife,
one I must learn to live within
my brushstrokes of sorrow,
hoping to find a place to
pigeonhole myself.

# THE FRUIT AND VEGETABLE GARDEN OF PAUL CEZANNE

Fine Vermeers three for $1!
Lots of Monet's misty water lilies
and Renoir's apple-cheeked girls
full-bosomed, plump as pears.

And Van Gogh's corn on the cob
straight from the field of crows.
Potato-men and their families
grubby arms and legs like roots.

Veggies diced like Velasquez, orange
rinds, glazed carrots, cherries,
Edam cheese and nuts on offer,
tomato grapes, and green peppers.

Dutch Masters at the dinner table
with plenty of green beans,
sugar snap peas like Irish eyes
opening like Georgia O Keeffe's.

# ODE TO GEORGIA O'KEEFFE

It seems nothing was too bold
beyond the brush.

Why not a tree with a torso?
You could hold or a liquid white
wishbone, blue radiation, the linear
made three-dimensional.

Why not a road that curved?
Like a pendulum's path to her
beloved home: ice palaces of
New York to Ghost Ranch.

Why not an embryo that breathed?
What canyon could stop her
in New Mexico or Manhattan
skyline full of stars?

Why not a flower like an ice flow?
Or orange glaciers where
she came to see herself
in all of these?

Why not a canvas of her making?
What dream was this, as prickly
as a Saguaro cactus, embodied
in a world of flesh?

Why not the crystal bowl of our being?
Why not the intelligence within
a skull or shell that looked inside
and opened all of us?

# PICASSO AT THE AGE OF 90

got up on a ladder
wearing nothing but
a pair of cut-offs
and with a liquid stroke

of his brush "whoosh"
painted on the wall
a perfect image of a
snow-white dove.

So will all of us leave
if not our imprint,
a carbon footprint
that will live in history,
our fossil of love.

# YEATS AT TWILIGHT

Imagine him with his sheep-dog look,
white-haired, rimless spectacles,
among the yew trees carving his name,
like he did in the autograph tree
in Coole Park at Lady Gregory's estate
with John Millington Synge.

The great poet swinging from a rope
swing in his widening gyre or playing
in the spray park, pants rolled up like
a newspaper as though he was gamboling
at the Gentleman's Bathing Beach outside
of Dublin, watching the waves making
water spouts.

Then he would speak to the Elms and Beeches
in the queerest high Irish tea-kettle voice, as though
he was invoking the faeries to go off gathering
chestnuts to take back to the Tower at Thoor Ballylee,
to warm himself around the great fire
of his Celtic Twilight.

And retiring back into his reveries, he'd dream
of Maud Gonne when he was young,
how he was an Irish senator and changed
the language with the ringing rock of his
oratory, full of prophecy of the coming times,
where in the vest of Celtic knots he would sleep
under Ben Bulben.

# THOMAS HARDY LISTENING TO JAZZ

Baby, it's cold outside and the leaves
are leaving their fingerprints on my windowsill.
O will o the wind!

Just take me back to those days
of scant sunlight, children playing out back.
What delight! I'd like to invite them in for tea.

There was a time when the softest moon
would appear, now we drink our beers
like cattle, shake our shaggy heads.

The death rattle is a wattle of what sticks
in our throat, those long-lost chicken bones.
Take a draught, holding those cold hands.

Now after the darkness yawns, I want to
go to bed, pull up the covers of the lawn
and sleep like a log in the potting shed.

Yes, baby, only six more hours of light
as I whistle through my missing teeth and
twirl the long silver ends of my mustache.

## SITTING AT THE SYLVIA BEACH MEMORIAL READING ROOM, AT SHAKESPEARE AND COMPANY, PARIS

At first the room is unnaturally quiet,
then a voice says: *You can take a book upstairs
from the library and read until midnight if you like.*
(It might have been the woman with red hair.)

So you climb the stairs dutifully just as others
must have done and the room is thick with dust
and the book jackets are all buttoned up, so
you pad in like an old retriever over the rug.

Mrs. Dalloway is the title you settle on, nearest
to your head, and then you sit down to read
in the green easy chair, as frayed
at the arm as your sweater. Hours pass.

Your eyes wander over the pages as you imagine
the neon light, the houseplant, and the bookshelves
leaning in to listen. Suddenly a thought is born:
*If no one discovers me here I could go blind as Milton.*

But no cause for alarm, there are only creaking floors
and a few chairs with lumbago—as long as the siren
you hear outside making an emergency call comes no
    closer.
Meanwhile, Mrs. Dalloway lives her life in a respectable
    way,
                        across the channel.

St. Michelle grows to an uproar, and the river rats of the
Seine begin to move as footsteps on the stairs, cracks
in the ceiling widen to a face. The curtain is continually
stirring as the words beneath your fingers rise from the
page in the needlepoint as lace.

# THE STARS THAT GOVERN US

*It is the stars, the stars above us, govern*
*our condition*

                         —*King Lear*

The stars are pinned against the sky,
pale and frozen in the ivory moonlight,
the constellations rigid as Monarchs.
Now become the dream: a human specimen.

Prod them with your eyes, let your fingers
trace the patterns of the Dipper's handle.
Drink deeply from the vessel's mouth;
how cold the moonlight feels on your tongue.

Turn it over, let the mercury run
down your veins until your body stiffens.
Arms and legs are turning in their sockets,
eyes light the way, turning like beacons.

Know that you're hollow to the core.
Feel the certain fusion of your hemispheres.
Your life is being pulled into its course,
piercing through your skin, the silver axis.

Your heart is hardening, feel its weight,
the valves are tightening slowly into place.
Now let them fix you with their icy stares;
now let them gaze at your great constellation.

# RUSSIAN DREAMS

Last night you slept in your cocoon,
covers pulled around you, three pillows
for your head, in your confetti
nightgown, red stars in celebration
as though you were in St. Petersburg
visiting the Winter Palace or Hermitage
the Nev was frozen solid.

While you were travelling through
Finland looking at the faces of the dead,
your eyes closed. Though you were only
passing through, you cozied up to me
your head against my shoulder
reading my mind the way you do.
I let you go on dreaming on that
train where nothing had changed,

hoping that when you awoke you
would still remember me by name.
There was so much light reflected
in your face from the snow, soft
enough to be alabaster white—
I thought it would bring you back
to me: my nesting doll!

# THE RAINBOW

It is what bridges us, light bending
as though to break, we wonder
at its dazzling arc,
how it shimmers by sunlight
curving the limits
of our space.
Its secret is more than alchemy:
no touch of gold could show how this sky transfixes
us.
Not even if our blood had become water
or the sea had turned our salt to tears
could we be more taken
than by this shining world.
But to see through our lives
is a trick we would sit still for.
There it doubles,
now it becomes three.
For here is light made
of air, sun, rain
leading us through
and one by one
or in pairs we follow it,
if only to be won over
at last by our blind belief,
so that with luck we might be shown the way
to our disappearing end.

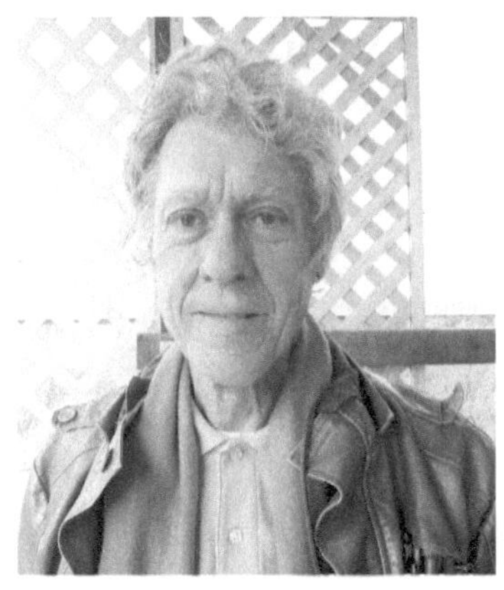

## ABOUT THE AUTHOR

Michael Magee's plays and poetry have been produced and published in the U.S., England, and Greece. His chapbooks include: *Ireland's Eye, A Trip to Jerusalem,* and the recently published *Dementia: Love is a Blur* and *Vanishing Points* (Beaux Arts Press, 2017). His play *Shank's Mare* was produced at Northwest Actor's Studio and later became a movie which won a best actor award at the Bare Bones, Script to Screen Film Festival in Tulsa, Oklahoma. *A Night in Reading Gaol With Oscar Wilde* was produced here and in Derby, England. He was co-editor of *2020 Tacoma: In Images and Verse* and is editor and publisher of Beaux Arts Press. Recent work has been published in *Cirque and Journal of Wild Culture.*

He has lived in Seattle, San Francisco, London, Nottingham, England and now lives in Tacoma, Washington. These poems are a culmination of work dating back to the 1970's when he was a student of David Wagoner and Bill Matchett at the University of Washington. He has written scripts

for radio and dance, won first prize in the Dancing
Poetry Contest in San Francisco and second prize
in *KindofaHurricainePress'* Editor's Choice Awards.
Michael has read at Shakespeare and Company, Paris
and on BBC Radio 1, as well as being a participant in
the Jack Straw Writer's Program for radio in Seattle.
He wrote several songs for the CD *Vaudeville.* He has
been an Artist-in-the-Schools in Washington, Seattle
Artist-in-Residence with the Seattle Arts Commission
and Arts and Aging Team. His first book: *Cinders of
My Better Angels* was published by MoonPath Press
in 2011 and was nominated for a Pacific Northwest
Bookseller's Award.

www.ingramcontent.com/pod-product-compliance
Lightning Source LLC
Chambersburg PA
CBHW022056050726
47591CB00002B/573